THIS WORLD

THE WESLEYAN POETRY PROGRAM : VOLUME 57

This World

POEMS BY

H A R V E Y S H A P I R O

Wesleyan University Press

MIDDLETOWN, CONNECTICUT

Paperback ISBN : 0–8195–1057–2

Hardbound ISBN : 0–8195–2057–8

Library of Congress Catalog Card Number : 72–142725

Manufactured in the United States of America

FIRST EDITION

TO EDNA

CONTENTS

IV

I

Now they are trying to make you
The genital thug, leader
Of the new black shirts —
Masculinity over all!
I remember you after the stroke
(Which stroke? I don't remember which stroke.)
Afraid to be left by Flossie
In a hotel lobby, crying out
To her not to leave you
For a minute. Cracked open
And nothing but womanish milk
In the hole. Only a year
Before that we were banging
On the door for a girl to open,
To both of us. Cracked,
Broken. Fear
Slaughtering the brightness
Of your face, stroke and
Counterstroke, repeated and
Repeated, for anyone to see.
And now, grandmotherly,
You stare from the cover
Of your selected poems —
The only face you could compose
In the end. As if having
Written of love better than any poet
Of our time, you stepped over
To that side for peace.
What valleys, William, to retrace
In memory, after the masculine mountains,
What long and splendid valleys.

DAYS AND NIGHTS

1.

You keep beating me down.
When I reach a balance,
You break it, always
Clawing for the heart.
In the electric light
We face each other.
Whatever you want of me,
Goddess of insomnia and pure form,
It's not these messages I scratch out
Morning after morning
To turn you off.

2.

Whether I had room
For all that joy
In my economy
Is another matter.
Rejecting me,
She shut out all my light,
Showed to me the backs
Of houses, tail lights
Going fast,
Smiles disappearing.
Every man
Was my enemy.
So it was for many a day.
I could not
Climb out of it,
So close was I
To her will.

3.

"He that is wise may correct natures."
Alchemy. The philosophical stone.
Your shadow over the page.
Your hair to my cheek.
Your eyes great riding lights
In the alcoholic storm that now
I remember, along with that
Bruising sweat of rhetoric
I thought appropriate to the times.
He that is wise
May have his life to remember.
But I am reduced to reciting
The letters of the alphabet.
If I say them with fervor
(Saying them with fervor)
Will memory be stirred?
Your own goddess-voice
In the leaves, in the night
Of the body, as I turn the page.

4.

Well, it was only Bottom's dream —
Methought I was and
Methought I had.
Outside, the sky is a field
In which the seeds of minerals shine.
And I am hunched over the board
On which I write my nights
Breathing configurations
On the winter air. As far from you
As ever I was far from you.

The cold locks everything in place.
Now I am here. The flame of my match
Everything that is given to me.

5.
Suddenly I see your face close up
And all my senses scramble
To get the shock
Home again. In sleep
Not knowing who I am
Or however that spent match struck.

6.
The white brilliance under the eyelids
So that all things appear to me
In that color. The worlds you see
Exist in joy. Eyes like doves.
Equilibrium, a white brilliance.

7.
Now you come again
Like a very patient ghost,
Offering me Zen records,
A discourse on the stomach
As the seat of the soul,
Your long white neck to kiss.
The tiger's eye that is
Your favorite jewel
Shines in your hand.
Wanting to, I can't conjure

You up, not a touch.
Unbidden, you cross a thousand miles
To say, This is the gift
I was going to give you forever.

THE LESSON

While other cases
Lean away from the nominative,
The poet is giving the girl
Large roses.
They are blood-red roses.
They require no prepositions
As they come through
To the girl, become
The girl's face and body;
And wholly blood-red
Are fixed in the nominative
Like a pulse.

The light is sown.
It is there, under the stones
That have been flung
On the street.
Behind my house now
It is in full flower.
The leaves of the mimosa
Are edged with light.
This is the gift
I have and do not claim.
If I could take
The world like that —
All things to which
The light adheres:
Your body edged with light
Which I claim
And count on
And lose
And claim again.

BY THE WOMEN'S HOUSE OF DETENTION

Love is the beggar's itch
And I depart
Past the stockaded women, tier on tier,
Singing the same song
Through their delicate home.

Sundays, the colored lesbians
Lean in the street and cry
Up to the latticed windows
Love's old sweet song.

Happy in these streets
I see out of some dark cellar
Orpheus lead Eurydice

While past me goes
Young Icarus, his red heart
Bleating like a sheep
In the fall from perpetual music.

This summer, like a jungle,
I dream in a confusion of chairs
As love over the ancient city
Flares like an angel's eye.

Sir Thomas Wyatt,
When she cries out
I hear her from my darkness.
Words collide
But what shakes me
Is her tongue
Coming to find.

THE ONLY LIVE ONE

Cardiac zombies
Under the Miami moon.
Memories of you
And your spade lovers
Coming in from the sea now —
That Buddha shake
You give to your head
When I look at you.
In the Himalayan hills
You've answered the phone.
I hear you say,
I'm real! I'm real!
The only live one
In the amphitheater of the sea.

We don't trust each other.
She says, we trust each other.
She gives me nothing.
I trust her, in that
Her fingers are long,
Her thighs are slim,
Her dark hair
Swings about her face.
I don't like
The pain, though
It's sweet.
I've had all that.
There's hardly a way
To speak about it.
Like Marvell's
Lovers we keep
Our stations.

GLORY

In the museum of antiquities
I ran my hands over
The breasts and thighs
Of the young Aphrodite
And heard her say, kiss my ass.

RECAPITULATIONS

1. Those were not salt tears.
   My mouth in your hand
   Appeared to be drinking.
   The words were lost.
   A drunken sleep.
   Only your turning to your name
   As I desperately say.

2. I was wearing those funny socks,
   Businessmen's hose,
   And dreaming you loved me.
   I was strung so tight
   And the socks were so free
   In your jeans, and your hair,
   And your twenty-one years.

3. Tell me I have the right
   To live among these images.
   High up on the building wall
   A niche for the image. For you
   Pan and the Nymphs,
   The inscription in Greek
   On that one. Stunned
   By their sun and silence
   I step carefully through traffic
   So as not to disturb the smile
   Where you have turned to stone.

4. Rain this night
   Falls on the past.
   That hard ground
   Doesn't catch a drop.

MINUTE BIOGRAPHY

He thought of himself
As in the service of a lady
Or of the moon.
Though in truth
He was in the service
Of a style that was
Trying to grow
Hands and feet
And so had need of him
And filled his life.

II

The kids outside are breaking bottles
Because they have bottles in their hands.
Thinking of marriage
Because the words have a target.
After dark the traffic
Makes a kind of undersong.
I close my eyes
And watch the nighttime ferries
Like lighted keyboards.
What they play upon
Stretches like romance,
Night, an American life.

DEAR WIFE

Your tears will silk the pillow
And raise a luxury of weeds.
When those weeds find my headstone
We are both at peace.

Now the room is silent.
The venom must have
Spilled to the next room.

ON HER RISING

The room fills with rheum,
The light with blight.
The yellow of daffodils
Gilds her gums.
Catarrh be her motion,
Hawking be her song.
Along her damp side's
The warmth of mould.

His castrating wife is at the controls.
Blue Max, she says,
Take off.
They take off, winging it for
Haiphong, Taipei,
The China Seas.
Miles below, the dolphins
Heave and soar. It's their jet
Trails that streak the blue.
Friend or foe, friend or foe,
She shouts.
The question doesn't apply,
He'd like to explain —
If the intercom would work
Or the picture were real
Or if he hadn't just stepped out.

The players cry
"Reason" in Hamlet
And it is a ghost.
My own face
Shuffles at the windowpane.
Whatever I look through
Is deception — clear as that
Ghostly player crying
"Reason" when I hear "Revenge."
And murder is loose
On the broad highway.
My family digging for
Shelter as I come home,
Saying,
I give you this gift
Of reason.

POEM FOR E

Please take
Your god damn
Etruscan head
Out of my dreams.

III

The first snow of winter
And in my early morning dream
You with one breast uncovered
Talk to me
Of the possibilities of life.

The cats don't know what to do.
They roam the house.
We're all trying
To perceive where
Our happiness lies.

Through the shutters and closed windows
I hear the crunch of tires.
Nothing in my life
Is as clear to me.

Silence
Like snow.
At forty-four
To be back
In the drifts!

FACING A WALL

1. I take up my position:
   To make sense of that wall.

2. When they say
   History doesn't matter,
   Do they mean lives?

3. Among these many voices,
   The voice of a friend,
   On the level.

4. Glacial.
   Nothing moves
   But the ice.

5. You are too dependent
   On what is placed before you:
   The sea, a sunset,
   A long life.

6. Without difficulty,
   To bring words
   Into this world.

7. In a country of trees
   Prepare the way for the desert.

1. What is it that I have to do?
   My body accuses me,
   The cause of its uselessness.
   My imagination
   Turns its pockets inside out.
   I explain everything
   At length
   And set it down.
   My need, I cry,
   My need. But you
   Walk away from it
   As if to say
   Ah, you're only trying
   To change your life.

2. I watch my life hour by hour.
   I call it a natural process,
   Even organic growth.
   Hidden in its proliferating
   Activities, mortgages, lusts
   There is a mind
   Probably tracing a shape.
   In moments of stress
   That mind seems to be watching me,
   Anxious for a response.
   Then I nod to show
   I am satisfied with the arrangement
   If it is.

3. We're all attached to our lives.
   Some strongly, some

By the thinnest of lines.
But at times
We seem to be floating
Or our lives floating
One from the other
In a great happiness.

My dead sister dreams away her life.
About forty years of dreaming
As I count.
My father blamed my mother
For the child's death
And wasn't at the funeral.
The tears, the tears she bred
In me out of my sister's loss,
Weeping of hurt, deprivation, age,
The insanity of life.
My sister, eager for her share,
Under such a tiny headstone
In a city we never pass.
Kin, dreaming dark poems
That spill into my life.

TO MY FATHER

Whatever it was
Illuminating me
With dreams

I saw your face
Words on your eyelids

Windows on all four sides
To let the light in

What would you do
With this body
You would die in it
Again
You would not even
Write these poems.

The children are taken with seizures of feeling.
We must learn to help them.
The mind must learn to help them.
It is like a song that begins
Sanely and ends savagely. Sing it with them
Pretending to be caught. Be anxious
About the space around you — can
It contain the song.
Nobody mourns like that any more.
Enjoy being your own colony.
The feelings are a colony. If you have to
Pretend there are words to the song,
There are words to the song.

SPACES

1. Quickening his step, my father
   Came into the room.
   Now I will tell you about myself,
   He said.
   When I write these words
   A torpor comes over me.
   I can hardly hold the pen.

2. If you want to become a wall,
   Work at it. More plaster, I mean,
   And more paint.
   Get the job done.

3. To be summoned like that
   Startles me.
   I put on the light
   At 2 AM
   And stand
   At the edge of a field.

4. Putting words
   To these sounds
   You have your own
   Victory.
   But to recognize it.

1. That the galaxy is a river of light
   That the order of seeds is in my hand
   I ask to enter this world without confusion.

2. The enormous lights
   And mysteries of this world
   Which the teacher says
   I shut from myself
   With a hand,
   Spending my sight
   On these snarled lines,
   This closed-in town
   Where I walk and work
   And find you in sleep
   In the dark room, the dark town,
   In a life that I cannot
   Honestly call the way.

3. He has been asking for help
   Everywhere for his child
   With the clogged tongue.
   Not that the boy
   Should speak with eloquence.
   But that he should speak
   His need — to the world,
   The citizens. The barest
   Speech. I am happy.
   I am sad.
   The sense is beautiful.

4. The reader begins
    With the destruction of the city.
    It is the same tune
    Every day for a week now.
    But how he appears to enjoy
    That rattle of words.
    Crowds fleeing, others
    Looting shops
    In the most expensive
    Avenues of the city.
    Smoke like a cowl
    Over the words
    And the reader's body.
    He must experience it
    To the end
    Each day, as it was set down
    From the roots of heaven.

5. In the sequence
    The angel of each verse
    Stands like a point of flame.

IV

FROM MARTIN BUBER

"A story must be told in such a way
That it constitutes help in itself."
Or not the way telephone addicts
Trap themselves for eternity
In a recital of symptoms —
Blood pressure, urine, sleep —
Saying tonight what they will
Relive tomorrow.

(Finding you whole
After a night of hatred
World to my touch
Like bread to my touch
Which I ceaselessly crumble
And the loaf is there.)

(Or when the traffic slurs
Early in the morning
Of a long night
And I strike it rich
With calm.)

THE SYNAGOGUE ON KANE STREET

Anachronisms are pleasant.
I like shifting periods
As the young rabbi doesn't shift tones
Saying "The Ethics of Maimonides"
And "The Reader's Digest."

There is no reason for survival.
As we drift outward
The tribal gods wave farewell.

It is the mother synagogue of Brooklyn.
We are a handful in a cathedral.

When I was asked
I said the blessing
For the reading of the scroll
Almost correctly.

The reader had a silver pointer.

The parchment before me
Was like a beginning.

RIVERSIDE DRIVE

from the Yiddish of Joseph Rolnick

Pulling myself out of bed,
I leave the house.
The blueness caresses me.
The wind pushes my hair.
A whole world of quiet
I fill with my steps
On the sidewalk,
And in the street,
The milkman's horse.
Somewhere, on a higher floor,
Along a dark corridor,
The milkman makes his shining rows.
Running, the papers
Under my arm,
I don't look at numbers.
I know the way
Like the horse.
The sun is already up
On the east side of the city.
Its flames, its grace
Spill, whole canfuls, on the cliffs
Of the Jersey shore.
At 310 Riverside Drive
A man on a low balcony,
Young but with mustache and beard —
His appearance not of here —
Stretches a hand toward
The west and shouts

Something like, See there!
And I stand like him
With my papers raised
Like an offering
To the light.
The two of us
Come for the first time
To this place,
To the red cliffs
Of this morning.

Where did the Jewish god go?
Up the chimney flues.
Who saw him go?
Six million souls.
How did he go?
All so still
As dew from the grass.

THE WAY

Why are you crying in Israel,
Brother, I ask as I switch over
To the emergency oxygen.
Do we have to dig up all
The Freudian plumbing
To reconstruct our lives?
If I had clean air like you
I think I could breathe.
As it is my mouthpiece keeps
Clogging and my eyes blur.
I can barely make it
Between the desks.
And you, walking
Between orange trees
Among the companions,
And still so far from the way.

Every morning I look
Into the world
And there is no renewal.
Every night, my lids clamped,
I concentrate
On the renewal to come.

I am on the lookout for
A great illumining,
Prepared to recognize it
Instantly and put it to use
Even among the desks
And chairs of the office, should
It come between nine and five.

KABBALAH

Keen as breath

Black as law

And heaven

Moving through darkness, clouds,
And thick darkness.
Returning through darkness, clouds,
And thick darkness.
Some lift up their heels
And some jump.

1. Souls from the world
   Of formlessness
   Are up before me,
   Moving through the house,
   Waiting for me
   To make the attempt
   (As I do each morning)
   Which they enjoy and nullify.

2. What are you looking for?
   Anything
   To bind the soul
   To its roots.

3. In the Book of the Revolutions of Souls
   Which we are now writing
   Willing or not.

   Tell me, declare the phantom
   Of your heart. The gods
   Are all equal.

   Every night climbing
   Out of that nothingness
   Into that nothingness.

A MESSAGE FROM RABBI NACHMAN

The extra-human
Swarms with disciples.
Like worms
Tumbling out of the Book of Creation,
The Book of Splendor.
Each with a light
In his head.
But smeared with
The contemplation of ecstasy.

Kabbalah —
A transmission
From mouth to ear.
The words of my friend
Steady my world
Even as I say them.

There are stones —
How else will the house
Be built —
Like souls
That are flung down
In the streets.

LINES FOR ERWIN R. GOODENOUGH (1893–1965)

"If Aphrodite could take Moses
From the ark in the Nile
In the synagogue at Dura"

Naked as she was
Her breasts blue-pointed

If Aphrodite could move
Among these sheols
Of the dead

If she to ornament the dark
Could bend her body
To the water
Promising life
From the mother

"Come down upon this cup which stands before me,
Fill it with grace and a holy spirit,
So that it becomes for me a new plant within me."

COUPERIN'S TENEBRAE

With my derby on,
A cigar. Listening
To that sweet voice.
Dead gods, old texts,
Layer under layer.
Armand is chasing
The music. I am
Chasing the music.
Nobody says
What to do
With those dead gods.
Keep my spirit clear,
I'll tell
Everything I know.

Battering at the door
Of a pretend house
With pretend cries
Of rage and loss
As I sit remembering
Quiet
And dead white.

CROSS COUNTRY

The night's traffic.
I can barely follow the markers,
My eyes stung with seeing.
Snow in the mountains
Is so beautiful.
All through the chemical wastes
Of New Jersey
I follow my guide —
Rare truths in the mountains —
While the kids
Sleep in the back with my wife.
No one to see me
For the dazzling snow.

FIELD MICE

Some wood notes are wild.
Glad to have you in the house,
Piteous small creatures.
Like mad English poets
Of the eighteenth century,
Something crying to be saved.

HELLO THERE!

for Robert Bly

> The poets of the midwest
> Are in their towns,
> Looking out across wheat, corn,
> Great acres of silos.
> Neruda waves to them
> From the other side of the field.
> They are all so happy
> They make images.

DEFINITIONS OF POETRY

1. A practical use
   Of mysterious names:
   Sun, night, morning, cloud,
   Illumination, dreams, love.

2. I want to get out of my skull
   For just a little while.
   I can't stand the fighting.

3. It's a profitless tit
   Said my wife as she put
   The baby down.

4. The mist of its own weight.
   This striving to wrestle
   Myself for a meaning,
   Someone must grow tired.

5. I saw myself walking there
   Like a bug walking on its shadow
   All the way to the dark.

6. The lions are sleeping now
   On either side of my forehead,
   Keeping the tension in sleep.

ON SOME WORDS OF BEN AZZAI

You will be called by your name.
You will be seated in your place.
You will be given what is yours.
The dream goes something like that
For everyone, I suppose, except
When it's happening and the world
Comes true, the air, the sky.
But all of yesterday and again today
I knew the dream. Age will end it.

1. Thinking that
   In the multiple
   Conclusions of a life
   There may be
   A line truthful
   Enough to hand on

   Against the attempt
   To create a culture
   I place the attempt
   To create a life.

   This morning
   I forgot all about
   The continuity
   Of American poetry
   Engaged on a national mission
   Without pay.

2. You think
   There must be more
   To it than this —
   A narrow examination
   Of a life
   A secret poring over books
   A listening
   For whatever stirs
   An intense listening.

3. Peace
   Goddess-voice
   Keep telling me a story.

A HISTORY

1. You say my thoughts are gestures.
   How many times a day
   Must I destroy the world?

2. Whatever must rescue me
   Will come from outside.
   It
   Strikes my forehead
   Now like the flat
   Of a hand.

3. Then it was the time
   To take myself seriously again

   To attack the others

   To fight for my life.

   The stink of non-being
   Was on my hands

   So I put them to work.

4. Like the fire engine speeding
   Out of the firehouse,
   The hoarse cry of the last men
   As they board her,
    As I stare into the wide night,
   The nothingness
   That gives life.

He is not strong enough
For his experience.
When he cries,
The cat stirs
At the foot of his bed
For a moment.

I tell him
The night's flow —
The traffic and street noises —
Carries sleep.

His dreams
Cannot contain
His experiences.

They go on about him
Like a war
And the poets
Cannot make sense of it.

What is it
That feeds winds and rivers
And the stars?

HOW THE NEWS REACHED ME

My older son was upstairs
Watching a rerun of D Day,
The cannons booming.
I was downstairs
In the dark
Watching the white roses
That had just bloomed —
June 1 — against the wall
Of the South Brooklyn
Settlement House.
It was my war
And I sensed it was over.

Because I felt the power
Of what I did not know,
Knew it
As my body tried
Not to know it,
Came that close
To the seizure of stone
And the regression of
Language, saying
The blunt sounds
In my dream
With iron hinges,
To the level floor
As I cross it,
Thanks and praise.
And want no other thing
Of darkness,
Prince of this world.

EVENTS

1. Nothing was known of those events,
   The unconscious appearances
   Of the self. Like tracking
   History on the sea's surface.

2. Facing the dark,
   Fortified by bourbon,
   The dreams already
   In my head.

3. The paranoia
   That makes him move.

The man was thrown clear
Yet the experts say
To stay in the car is best.
To tap an undercurrent of
Feeling, something I turn away
From, fearful, certain
It will end but not knowing
How it will end.
The dreams have a childish
Beauty. Fireplaces, planes,
Tractors to clear the roads.

THE ARGUMENT

All right, there are thrones upon thrones.
There is suffering and redemption.
There is exile and return.
But to myself, gripping this pavement?
Thrones upon thrones.
You keep placing them there,
Pyramiding them there
In a golden game.
Art and imagination.
But on this pavement,
In this life, with these eyes?

ALL RIGHT, DOGEN

I let fall
My body and my mind
Into the street,
Watch the world
As pure object
Come back
Like a fist.

IT IS

The smell of enlightenment
Meaning:
I have been there
Before
And brought nothing
Back.

It's a continuity tape
Of the harbor and the bridge
And my life walking past.

In your true and terrible form,
Angel of this world.

FOR DELMORE SCHWARTZ

1.

How do they go on living?
How does anyone go on living?
A woman kills her three children
In 1954. In 1966 she kills
Another three. And the husband
Continues to go to work
At the same job. Which
Is to be judged insane?
And we keep walking the same
Roads, past mayhem, slaughter
Of innocents — this morning, the granny
Curled up beside her bottle
Of Petri wine at a side door
Of the Paramount — every day,
Leading sensible lives.
The sirens seem never to stop,
Even in the country, amid
Crickets or ocean sound.
What we all know,
What keeps humming in the back
Of the brain. When the language
Pauses, the killing begins.

2.

Your intelligence was so clear
In your first poems, like
Mozart in his music.
Yet it could not help you,
As you said,
When the old arguments,
The din around the family table,
Grew louder all about you —
The arguments we endlessly rehearse
When mind loses its own motion.
Then our jaws lock into the face
We had, on the words we said
Under our breath, to ourselves,
To our underselves, so fiercely deep
They were for years beyond hearing,
And now do all the talking.

3.
Disturbed by dreams,
I wake into the chilled morning.
The dreams are rich
With patterns of rejection
(Mother, Wife) suicide and loss.
A victim of such disasters,
When I awake I judge myself
Harshly and long.
Four AM on a vacation morning.
The surf takes over in my head, a running
Commentary, a Greek chorus,
Saying something like, nothing but the sea.
In my universe of feeling,
I can hear the sea. These dreams,
Bits of genre, Viennese pastry,
From which I awake, stuffed
With bourgeois living, these dreams
Of the dead fathers I believe in . . .